Christmas in Paris and the Provinces

Parisians celebrate the winter
holiday season as they skate at
the Place de l'Hôtel-de-ville.

Christmas in Paris and the Provinces

— ●

Christmas Around the World
From World Book

World Book, Inc.
a Scott Fetzer company
Chicago

Staff

Executive Committee

President
  Paul A. Gazzolo
Vice President and Chief
  Marketing Officer
  Patricia Ginnis
Vice President and Chief
  Financial Officer
  Donald D. Keller
Vice President and Editor in Chief
  Paul A. Kobasa
Director, Human Resources
  Bev Ecker
Chief Technology Officer
  Tim Hardy
Managing Director,
  International
  Benjamin Hinton

Marketing

Director, Direct Marketing
  Mark R. Willy
Marketing Analyst
  Zofia Kulik

Editorial

Associate Director,
  Supplementary Publications
  Scott Thomas
Managing Editor,
  Supplementary Publications
  Barbara A. Mayes
Manager, Research,
  Supplementary Publications
  Cheryl Graham
Senior Editor
  Kristina Vaicikonis
Manager, Contracts and Compliance
  (Rights and Permissions)
  Loranne K. Shields
Manager, Indexing Services
  David Pofelski
Administrative Assistant
  Ethel Matthews

Editorial Administration

Director, Systems and Projects
  Tony Tills
Senior Manager, Publishing Operations
  Timothy Falk

Graphics and Design

Associate Director
  Sandra M. Dyrlund
Associate Manager, Design
  Brenda B. Tropinski
Associate Manager, Photography
  and Digital Media
  Tom Evans
Contributing Photographs Editor
  Carol Parden
Manager, Cartographic Services
  Wayne K. Pichler
Coordinator
  Matt Carrington

Production

Director, Manufacturing
  and Pre-Press
  Carma Fazio
Manufacturing Manager
  Steven K. Hueppchen
Production/Technology Manager
  Anne Fritzinger
Production Specialist
  Curley Hunter
Proofreader
  Emilie Schrage

The editors wish to thank all the members of the
Alliance française-Maison française de Chicago who
helped with the development of this publication. We
also wish to acknowledge the French Cultural Services
for research assistance throughout the project.

Text consultant

Réal de Mélogue
Directeur-Général de l'Alliance française
Maison française de Chicago
Chicago, Illinois

Food and crafts consultant

Marcelle M. Devane
Chairman, Groupe folklorique de l'Alliance française-
Maison française de Chicago
Worth, Illinois

World Book, Inc.
233 N. Michigan Ave.
Chicago, IL 60601
Printed in the United States of America
1 2 3 4 5 12 11 10 09 08

**For information on other World Book publications,
visit our Web site at www.worldbook.com or call
1-800-WORLDBK (967-5325). For information about
sales to schools and libraries, call 1-800-975-3250
(United States) or 1-800-837-5365 (Canada).**

Library of Congress Cataloging-in-Publication Data
Christmas in Paris and the provinces.
    p. cm. -- (Christmas around the world)
    Summary: "Customs and traditions of the Christmas holidays
as celebrated in Paris and the provinces of France. Includes crafts,
recipes, and carols"--Provided by publisher.
    ISBN 978-0-7166-0812-7
    1. Christmas--France--Paris. 2. Christmas--France.
3. Paris (France)--Social life and customs. 4. France--Social
life and customs. I. World Book, Inc.
GT4987.48.C49 2009
394.26630944'361--dc22
                                          2008032219

Contents

*Thousands of twinkling lights
along the Champs-Élysées illuminate
the Arc de Triomphe in Paris as
Noël comes to France.*

Noël Comes to France

Noël! The lovely French word for Christmas literally means "the birthday of Christ." And the people of Paris, the capital of France, and all of the provinces celebrate it with deep devotion. Noël is observed throughout the land with beautiful midnight Masses, charming manger scenes, and countless reenactments of the Nativity.

Signs that Noël is approaching begin to appear in most areas of France soon after December 6, the feast day of Saint Nicholas, and continue through January 6, the Epiphany. The entire winter holiday season is a joyous one of merrymaking, gatherings with family and friends, Christmas decorations, and delicious holiday foods.

But Noël itself is a celebration for children. The French cherish childhood as a time of innocence to be safeguarded for as long as possible. A child filled with Christmas wonder and joy is a sacred reminder of the innocence of the Christ Child whose birthday is commemorated. For grownups, preparing for Christmas is like recapturing one's own childhood of long ago.

A flower vendor offers bunches of mistletoe to shoppers at her stall in the Quai aux Fleurs, near the Cathedral of Notre Dame, in Paris.

Trees in the flower stalls

The French know Christmas is near when they begin to see *sapins de Noël,* or Christmas trees, at the outdoor flower markets, standing in fragrant rows like miniature forests. Although Christmas trees are not quite as popular in France as they are in Germany, the United Kingdom, and the United States, the practice of putting up a tree at Christmastime is still widespread.

The trees come in all sizes, from tall and bushy to table-top size, the better to fit into a small apartment. Whichever type, the trees very often will be potted. The French are a practical people, and potted trees not only last longer, they may be replanted outdoors after the holidays are past.

It is often a challenge to select just the right tree, but carrying it home can be a problem. Trying to stuff a stubborn fresh tree into an automobile—or, worse still, into a taxi—can stretch one's patience. But the French can be seen doing both as Noël draws near.

The flowers of Noël

In addition to Christmas trees, French outdoor flower markets and flower shops offer a wealth of other decorations for the home. There are branches of fir, both plain and flocked, and prickly boughs of holly. Mistletoe is almost a Christmas necessity, appearing in great bunches. The custom goes back to the ancient Celts, some of whom lived in the area that is now France.

The Celts believed that mistletoe, with its shiny, waxy berries and dusky evergreen leaves, symbolized immortality. It was also thought to have miraculous powers of healing. The Celtic priests treated the plant with great reverence.

The mistletoe they sought often grew high at the top of great oak trees. The priests cut the boughs down with a golden sickle and never allowed them to touch the ground. As the boughs dropped, they were caught below in a pure white cloth.

Today, the French consider mistletoe a good luck charm. Young men and women have an even better reason for liking it. Hung in branches around the house, often tied with a red ribbon, the festive plant provides an excellent opportunity for claiming a holiday kiss.

In some areas, mistletoe is gathered on Christmas Eve and then brought back to decorate the house or, in the country, the stable.

Of all Christmas decorations, however, the most important are flowers. No French host or hostess considers the holiday table complete without a lavish arrangement of some kind. Guests bring flowers, too, as a gesture of thanks. Roses, gladioli, carnations, and snapdragons are favorite Christmas choices, along with a wide variety of dried flowers. Potted plants are also popular: red and white poinsettias, sweet-smelling hyacinths, multicolored azaleas, and Christmas begonias.

Political divisions called departments replaced French provinces (names in red, above) more than 200 years ago. However, many of the people of France still identify strongly with the traditional province in which they live or in which they were born.

Rose de Noël

A favorite Christmas flower in parts of France is the hellebore, which is often called the Christmas rose.

In some parts of France, a very special flower graces the Christmas table. It is called the hellebore—a blossom with creamy white petals, glossy leaves, and a dark green stem. The French call it the Christmas rose, or rose de Noël.

There is a legend about how this flower came to be and how it got its special name. The story tells about a young bellringer named Nicaise, who lived in a village near Rouen in the north of France. Nicaise was dull-witted. His guardian, a poor parish priest named Father Anthime, frequently scolded him for the foolish things that Nicaise did. Once on Christmas Eve, after an especially severe scolding, Nicaise sadly went up into the church tower until it was time to ring the bells for the midnight Mass. He soon fell fast asleep.

The church tower was ornamented with several ugly gargoyles, stone rainspouts carved to look like horrible beasts with their tongues sticking out. As Nicaise slept, he dreamed one of the gargoyles came to life.

The gargoyle spoke to him, saying that it was actually the Devil. The gargoyle told Nicaise that it liked him, which pleased the boy. (Remember, Nicaise was not terribly bright.)

Then the gargoyle offered Nicaise three wishes. Nicaise thought a bit. Finally, he said: "I'd like to be smart, that's one. And rich, that's two. And married to a beautiful lady. That's three."

The gargoyle agreed. Then Nicaise remembered that it was Christmas, and there were no flowers to decorate Father Anthime's little church.

"Please," he begged. "I also want some flowers for Father Anthime to place at the altar tonight."

The gargoyle spat with rage. That was too much. It told Nicaise to make do with what he already had been given. And the gargoyle added that it expected a little something in return. It demanded Nicaise's soul.

The gargoyle told the boy that it would return in one year's time to take him away. "Unless," it laughed nastily, "on Christmas Eve one year from now, you can make flowers bloom in the snow!"

Nicaise woke up. What a strange dream, he thought. But was it really a dream? For as the months went by, all three wishes came true.

The full year passed, and it was once again Christmas Eve. Nicaise knew the Devil was coming for him that night. Fright-

ened, he confessed his sins to Father Anthime.

The priest was horrified. "You've sold your soul," he cried, "and the Devil's coming to get you this very night—unless, by some miracle, you can actually make flowers bloom in the snow outside. My son, pray. Pray to the Good Lord, the angels, the saints, and to our Lord Jesus!"

The two knelt and prayed together as the midnight hour approached. Finally, thinking that the end was near, Nicaise crept sadly up the stairs to ring the bells one last time.

Just as he started to reach for the bell rope, he heard a cry from down below. Some children had wandered into the small church garden and they had found, of all things, flowers in the snow! Father Anthime came running, and when he saw the flowers, he began to weep.

"Nicaise," he called. "Come down, you are saved! We have won against the Devil. The Christ Child has sent flowers, real flowers—Christmas roses—to bloom in the snow!"

Shoppers in Paris (top) and Strasbourg (bottom) enjoy selecting new Christmas ornaments to adorn their trees. Christmas markets operate during the holiday season in cities throughout France.

Trimming the tree

Many French families own dozens of ornaments that they have collected over the years, but it is always fun to shop for new ones. Special stalls in the outdoor markets sell them, as do department stores. There are rows upon rows of shimmering baubles: shiny globes, frosted and plain, graceful bells in glowing colors, exotic birds, tiny angels, and replicas of Père Noël, the French Father Christmas.

Children love the small knitted or crocheted figures of animals, elves, and stars. There is tinsel, too, in gold and silver. Even paper fish are sometimes sold as Christmas ornaments. They represent the golden carp, once a symbol of long life. Today, the fish is a symbol of the New Year.

The tree is usually decorated a week to a few days before Christmas. The entire family participates, especially the children. The littlest ones help place ornaments, and perhaps gilded pine cones and walnuts, on whichever branches they can reach. Sometimes, with the help of an adult, they make paper flowers, stars, or swans. These are hung with great care. At the top of the tree, Maman or Papa may place a star, an image of Père Noël, or perhaps a treasured angel. Tinsel garlands add the finishing touch.

Most French families adorn their trees with colored or white electric lights. Often the hearth is decorated, too, with ornaments, paper garlands or bunches of red ribbon, and candles.

Displaying the crèche

By far, the most important symbol of French Christmas is the *crèche,* or manger scene. Churches set up their crèches sometime in the weeks preceding Christmas. Many crèches are magnificent, ornate displays; others are merely simple groupings of the Holy Family. More than 1 million visitors each year visit the crèche at the Cathedral of Notre Dame in Paris. There, they are encouraged to leave a message of peace in an urn beside the manger.

To children, the crèche is both a small world of fantasy and the focus of their devotion to the story of Christ's birth. The home crèche is set up a few days before Christmas, along with the tree. It is placed in a corner of the living room, on a table, or sometimes near the hearth.

Delicate porcelain figures grace a crèche in Bayonne, in southeastern France.

Some families may have antique crèche figures. These are often passed down from generation to generation, carefully preserved, and brought out only when it is time to set up the scene. Other families have simple manger scenes, with only a few figures. Imagination and personal taste are the two most important factors in how the crèche is presented.

Miniature figures for the crèche are also sold in department stores and in booths at the outdoor markets. On display are small images of Joseph and Mary, angels, shepherds, and the Three Wise Men, which the French call the Three Kings. No matter how many crèche figures a family may already have, there is always room for more. New additions may be purchased each year to replace worn or broken ones or to add a new dimension to the scene.

In the southern region of Provence, moss and pine boughs are needed, too, to use as background for the crèche. Children traditionally make a special trip to the woods and fields a few days before Christmas to find the materials. There they gather the moss and branches, plus handfuls of small stones. Later at home, the family will make the scene as real as possible. A length of deep-blue cloth may become the nighttime sky; a small mirror may become a miniature lake.

Often, children will have made other items for the scene: cardboard farm buildings, a small papier-mâché bridge, or a hill or two. The tiny crèche figures are placed as realistically as possible. Villagers are either on their way to the manger or busy at their usual jobs: sawing wood, drawing water from the well, or perhaps sitting around a bubbling cooking pot. Shepherds huddle around a tiny fire made from red tin foil; the Three Kings seem to move closer to the manger as Christmas Eve approaches.

Many churches and cathedrals, including the Strasbourg Cathedral (top), set up a traditional crèche several days before Christmas. Children in Provence (above) gather moss, stones, and branches with which to adorn a family crèche.

After all the figures are arranged, moss, stones, or pine boughs are added for a final touch of authenticity. Fluffy snow for a winter scene is created with flour from the kitchen or with cotton. Finally, the crèche is complete, except for one figure: the tiny Infant Jesus. The manger remains empty until Christmas Eve, for it is not until then that the Christ Child will be born.

The wheat of Saint Barbara

In some areas of France, especially the region of Aquitaine and the province of Provence, the Christmas season begins on December 4, with the feast of Saint Barbara. Such a saint was not mentioned in historical references before the 600's. However, legend has it that Barbara was a young Christian woman who lived in the late 200's. Her father was not a Christian, and when Barbara refused a non-Christian suitor he had chosen for her, her father had Barbara brought before a judge, who sentenced her to be beheaded. She is often depicted holding a sheaf of wheat.

On the feast of Saint Barbara, children wrap a grain of wheat in a damp bit of cloth or cotton and place it in a saucer on a windowsill to germinate. If it sprouts and grows, it is a sign of good luck in the coming year for all in the household. The children carefully tend the green shoot throughout the Christmas season. On the eve of Noël, it may be tied with a ribbon and placed in the crèche or used as a decoration for the Christmas Eve dinner.

The Feast of Saint Nicholas

As the preparations for Noël progress, many communities observe a number of other rituals as well. Children—particularly those in the eastern provinces of Alsace and Lorraine—eagerly anticipate Saint Nicholas Day on December 6, for it means gifts of candy and other goodies. (In other areas of France, Saint Nicholas may bring gifts on Christmas Eve.)

Saint Nicholas was a bishop in Asia Minor (an area now part of Turkey) in the A.D. 300's. It is believed that he performed many miracles. He became the patron saint of sailors, scholars, clerks, bankers, and children. According to legend, Saint Nicholas once performed a miracle in which he brought three small boys back to life. A wicked, greedy innkeeper had killed the children and placed their bodies in a barrel of brine.

Saint Nicholas is also the patron saint of Lorraine. There, his feast day is celebrated as a major festival. Each year, processions

Children throughout France eagerly await December 6 for the arrival of Saint Nicholas, depicted in a statue in the Basilica of St.-Nicolas-de-Port in Lorraine.

wind through the old, narrow streets of the province's towns and villages, led by one or more men dressed up to represent the saint. The men carry crosses and wear mitres, the tall, pointed headgear worn by bishops. Behind them comes a cart, holding a barrel and images of the three rescued boys of legend.

There may also be another character walking in the procession. He is Père Fouettard, whose name in French means Father Whipper. Père Fouettard is an ugly, mean-spirited figure. He wears a long, dirty, dark-colored robe and a gray, poorly groomed beard. Instead of a sack of goodies, Père Fouettard carries an armload of switches.

Elaborate lighting is projected onto the Cathédrale Saint-Jean as part of the Festival of Light, which attracts thousands of visitors to Lyon annually on December 8.

Since at least the Middle Ages (about the 400's through the 1400's), Père Fouettard's task traditionally was to punish children who had not behaved well during the year by spanking them. By contrast, Saint Nicholas rewarded the good children with gifts. (Today, French parents tend to place less emphasis on Pére Fouettard as a punisher of children.)

The Festival of Light

In the city of Lyon, December 8 is also a very special day. On that day, thousands of people flock to the city to celebrate the Festival of Light—Fête de la Lumière. The Festival of Light commemorates the day in 1852 that the people of the city erected a statue to the Virgin Mary, for saving them from a plague that was raging outside the city gates. The people of Lyon placed candles in their windows as a tribute to Mary. Today, the fête has become a four-day celebration. The city is lit with thousands of lights, many of them hung in strands outlining the facades of historic buildings in the city. Torches, laser beams, projected image displays, and fireworks culminate in a light show over the Rhone River on December 8.

The festivities of Noël

Throughout the Christmas season, a holiday trip past the square next to the Georges Pompidou National Center of Art and Culture in Paris may find street musicians entertaining the crowds. Performing groups come to the square, too, including mimes, who amuse onlookers with their silent pantomime routines. In between performances, the actors in their clownlike costumes and painted faces may offer flowers to passers-by.

At the Cathedral of Notre Dame, the Nativity story is presented each year by regional groups from all over France. The city sponsors the performances, and admission is free. Men and women wear native costumes and sing traditional carols, many going back to the Middle Ages. Some shows may be simple choral presentations or carols mixed with regional dances. Others are modern interpretations of medieval Christmas plays set to music. These performances, called *pastorales,* are loaded with local humor and are often sung or spoken in the performers' native dialects. Pastorales are performed today in many regions of France, in community theaters, concert halls, and churches.

Provence, in southern France, particularly, specializes in Christmas Eve processions of shepherds who reenact the Nativity story with carols and music. Local townspeople act out the roles just as their forebears did in medieval days. Live animals—including oxen, donkeys, horses, lambs, and

Amateur actors wearing traditional regional dress perform a Nativity play at the Cathedral of Notre Dame.

sheep—sometimes play a part in the proceedings as well.

The processions are enormously popular, both among the local residents and the tourists who flock to the area to see them. The spectacles often end with a living crèche, where townspeople represent the manger figures. In some places, the Christ Child is portrayed by a real infant.

Families pause to enjoy a magician's performance while shopping at a Christmas market on the Place Saint Sulpice in Paris.

French children have a two- or three-week holiday from school at Christmastime. Some families go off to France's snowy Alpine regions for skiing, sledding, and tobogganing. A few head south to the warm Riviera. But there is plenty to do to keep everyone occupied right at home.

Preparing the home

In addition to attending Christmas performances and generally decorating for the holiday, preparing for Noël in some parts of France also means cleaning the house until it sparkles. In earlier times, housewives scurried about in a frantic rush to have everything spotless by Christmas Eve. In Sologne, in central France, the harried woman traditionally had to sweep the chimney. Then she swept the house, working from the walls and corners in, finishing up in front of the chimney. She also scrubbed the tiles and, finally, baked and cooked.

Modern families go about the housework in a more leisurely way, but dusting and waxing still need to be done, the family's finest china and silver must be brought out and polished for the Christmas meal, and all of the wonderful holiday foods must be prepared. The smells of good things to eat blend with the sharper odors of wax and furniture polish and the piney scent of the Christmas tree to become the distinctive fragrance of Noël.

The magic of shopwindows

Toy shopping is an exciting part of the pre-Christmas preparations. The oldest and most luxurious toy shop in Paris, Au Nain Bleu (the Blue Dwarf), has been offering toys to make any child happy at Christmas since 1836. Fashion dolls with couture clothing and toy wooden boats to sail in the Tuilleries fountains have given way to more modern—but no less exciting—choices.

Two of the largest and most prestigious department stores in Paris—Galeries Lafayette and Printemps Paris—are neighbors along Boulevard Haussmann. Each year, the stores' designers try to outdo each other with lavish decorations and window displays created just for the Christmas season. Their magical animated figures and elegant mannequins dressed in the height of winter fashion attract window shoppers from all over the world.

At Printemps Paris, several of the windows are adorned especially for children. And to make it easier for the young onlook-

Each year, two of the largest department stores in Paris, Galeries Lafayette (below, left) and Printemps Paris (below, right), try to outdo each other with elaborate holiday displays.

ers, the windows have ramps that children can climb to get a better look at the spectacular displays. Each year, the windows showcase the work of famous fashion designers in a fantasy winter setting. At Galeries Lafayette, the store's facades are outlined with millions of multicolored lights that illuminate the boulevard. The displays are unveiled in mid-November and remain on exhibit until the end of December.

Inside, where it is warm, Printemps Paris offers a one-of-a-kind Christmas gift shop, Boutique Noire (the Black Boutique). Here, gift buyers can find luxurious items that are available nowhere else in Paris. The store offers spectacular pieces of art, candles selected by designers and perfumers in hundreds of scents, and other innovative gifts.

There are enchanting seasonal scenes at various specialty shops, as well. Slinky mannequins may grace the windows at the boutique of Christian Dior, the famed dress designer. Similarly, Pierre Cardin, the shop for men, and Louis Vuitton are all decked out for the holidays.

France is known not only for its superb champagne but also for its perfumes. They, too, are displayed with matchless elegance. In the perfume department of the Galeries Lafayette, imposing arrays of exquisitely packaged scents may be found arranged under a great roof of twinkling white lights.

Chauds les marrons!

Buying Christmas gifts, taking in the store window displays, or enjoying a performance by street musicians can leave a shopper cold and hungry. It's time for some hot chestnuts! Hot chestnut sellers can be found in stalls or carts along many streets and squares in France at Christmastime, the time of year the nuts are in season. Vendors grill the chestnuts in a charcoal brazier, and when they are ready, call out "Marrons! Chauds, chauds les marrons! ("Chestnuts! Hot, hot chestnuts!") They sell the chestnuts in paper bags or newspaper cones, ready to eat. Be careful not to burn your fingers as you peel the brown skin from the hot, roasted nut inside!

Delectable chocolates are another French specialty. Candy shops offer glorious displays of luscious sweets, unadorned or wrapped in rainbow shades of foil.

In one display, a shopper may find the humble wooden shoe refashioned in dark chocolate and filled with small hard candies, each wrapped in crinkly colored paper. In another, great pyramids of foil-wrapped candies challenge the most persistent sweet tooth.

A worker at a candy factory adds the finishing touches to a foot-high figure of Père Noël.

At night, the glittering lights of decorated streets reflect in the display windows of the shopping districts, magnifying the radiance. Most streets in France have only tiny white lights to herald the winter holidays. There are strings of white, globes of white, bells of white, candles of white—all adding to the splendor of the season.

In the west of France, there is more color in the outdoor decorations. Large red candles are a favorite, made up of dozens of small electric lights and tipped with a flame of shining yellow.

Waiting for Père Noël

But it would be a mistake to think that Christmas to the French is all glitter and glow. Though the shopping districts may sport a holiday costume, the home keeps its simple dress, and the daily routine goes on.

There are some who would insist, however, that the household atmosphere is a little more orderly, as the children prepare for a visit from Père Noël.

The children of France, like those of many lands, are never sure until Christmas morning whether they have been good enough all year to deserve gifts from the Christmas Spirit. Certainly, any French child with serious doubts will make a special effort to be polite and helpful as the big night approaches.

Most French children must also take care of one last, important detail. They write carefully composed letters to Père Noël, such as this one:

Dear Père Noël,

My name is Régine Wargny and I live in Villeneuve on Fère près de Château-Thierry, in Aisne. Since it will soon be Christmas, I am writing to you to tell you that I would love for you to bring me a big doll with long blond hair and a pretty dress, and also I would love some chocolates. This year I have been very good and I have worked well at school. I have never been punished. Christmas Eve, I will put my nice shoes and some beet greens for your donkey to one side of the tree.

I hope that it will not be too cold and that you will not catch a cold while giving out the gifts. I thank you for what you are going to send me.

Affectionately,
Régine

A boy posts his little sister's letter to Père Noël in plenty of time for Christmas.

The letters are mailed to Père Noël at the North Pole. On the way to the mailbox, there is the possibility that some lucky children might actually see Père Noël himself! He does not appear in France as commonly as Santa Claus does in the United States and Canada, but occasionally he may show up in a department store.

After their letters to Père Noël are mailed, French children find it difficult to wait for Christmas Eve. The great night always comes, however, and youngsters' patience is well rewarded. Noël—what a time for the children of France!

All is ready for the Christmas Eve supper, the réveillon.

Réveillon: The Holiday Feast

The Christmas holiday in France is observed in many ways—and especially in the preparation of exquisite foods. One of the grandest meals of the entire year is served at Christmas: the Christmas Eve "supper," called the réveillon. It is much more than just a simple supper, though. It is a lavish spread of delicious foods, course after course—all prepared in the fine tradition of French cooking.

The cuisine of France, renowned the world over, has come a long way since the days of Charlemagne, king of the Franks. In his time—the late 700's and early 800's—dinner was usually a large piece of meat or fish cooked on a spit. It was not until the 1300's that food in France began to receive any special treatment at all. When it did, dining (at least in the royal houses) became an occasion of magnificent splendor, notably at Christmastime. Chefs vied with one another to serve spectacular dishes, including creations called *sotelties*. Made of pastry or spun sugar, they depicted miniature castles, Biblical scenes, flowers, or exotic birds and beasts.

A shopper on Christmas Eve in Provence carefully chooses provisions for the 13 desserts she will serve during réveillon.

French cuisine became an art in the late 1600's, during the reign of King Louis XIV. He employed more than 50 chefs and lesser kitchen helpers in his royal residence at Versailles. Some of France's fabulous sauces were introduced at Louis XIV's table, as were *pâtés*—meat spreads, frequently of liver—and other delicacies. And, instead of massive quantities of the highly spiced and sweetened foods from previous eras, smaller portions featuring the natural flavors of foods were offered.

Shopping for réveillon

Interest in superb cuisine has never lessened in France. Today, restaurants, large or small, serve marvelous food, and French housewives pride themselves on their cooking. At Christmastime, they outdo themselves.

There is no one traditional réveillon dinner in France. The courses vary widely, according to the region. But whatever the locale, the meal will offer the very best of French cuisine.

To prepare for it, the French go shopping shortly before Christmas Eve. The task is not a matter of running into a supermarket and loading up a cart with packaged items. Shopping takes time and a good deal of effort, for only the highest quality foods—and the freshest—are acceptable.

In France, food is usually purchased over several days from individual shops or market stalls. The French set forth with their shopping carts or shopping bags to visit a long list of specialty shops.

They may begin at the fruit stalls. These are gorgeous sights with their colorful pyramids of oranges, apples, bananas, grapes, pears, tangerines, and plums. The French like their fruit very ripe, so that it may be peeled with a butter knife. The selection is a careful one.

The *boucherie,* or butcher shop, could come next. There, the shopper selects a roast of beef, a leg of lamb, or a plump goose, chicken, turkey, or duck. Such exotic delicacies as wild boar or venison are also available.

In the country, there are open-air fowl markets. The scene is a noisy one, with live geese and ducks waddling about loose or in pens, defiantly honking and quacking at passers-by. Ducks and geese already killed and plucked may hang stiffly in the background, sometimes on a string in two's or three's or more. Pheasants, still in their gorgeous plumage, tiny quails, and grouse may also be offered for sale. Vendors wait patiently for interested buyers or chat with friends. Sometimes an old dog lies dozing by the side of its master, peacefully ignoring all the commotion.

Next, one might visit the *pâtisserie,* or pastry shop. The highlight of Christmas dinner in France is the *bûche de Noël,* a cake shaped like a log. It is a latter-day, edible version of the ancient yule log. Pâtisseries offer all kinds of bûches, covered in dark or light chocolate, or even white chocolate tinted in many colors.

Basically the bûche is a sponge cake rolled with chocolate

Shoppers select their favorite bird from among turkeys, chickens, ducks, and geese at a poultry market in Réalmont, in southcentral France.

butter cream filling. Then it is frosted, and the brown icing is marked with lines, making it look like real bark. Sometimes extra pieces of cake have been added under the frosting, as bumps that resemble tree knots for even more realism. Then the log is decorated with confectioners' sugar, nuts, little images of Père Noël, sugar roses or real roses, elves, or perhaps sprigs of fresh holly.

Serving a bûche de Noël is so traditional at Christmas that it sometimes even appears in other forms. Recipes are printed in French magazines each year suggesting substitutes, such as a bûche made of layers of puréed carrots, spinach, and other vegetables, jelled and molded into a log. Or, there is a bûche of chilled pâté, frosted with a layer of rendered fat.

Along with the bûches de Noël, most pastry shops offer luscious trays of *tartes,* or pies, tartlets, petits fours, napoleons, éclairs, and all the other delectable pastries devised by the French. Often there will be a special display showing off the pastry maker's skill—such as a sleigh with Père Noël inside—all made from pastry, chocolate, and icing.

Another shop on the list is the *poissonnerie,* the fish shop. Silvery rows of fish of all kinds are on display, captured from the seas or from freshwater streams and rivers. Next are shellfish: snails, sea urchins, shrimps, clams, and mussels. Lobster is a favorite choice for the réveillon. Oysters, too, are traditional in many families.

Pâtés in many varieties are an important part of the réveillon. They are often purchased at the *charcuterie,* a unique kind of shop offering not just pâtés but all manner of prepared foods to take home: roast chickens and salads, snails in garlicky breadcrumbs, glazed hams, and trout or salmon in aspic. Occasionally, in the window a whole piglet is on display, boned, stuffed, cooked, and sold by the slice.

A pastry chef ices gingerbread figures that may be placed under a tree or inside a hopeful child's slipper on the family hearth.

Many people associate pâtés only with goose livers, but there are many kinds. Some are of rabbit or of duck mixed with minced ham or pork. They may appear *en croûte*, or baked in a shell of pastry. They are all to be eaten with bread and tiny sour pickles to complement the delicate flavor of the pâté.

Cheeses in all shapes, sizes, and smells are on sale at the charcuterie, too, and in other shops or stalls. A large disk of Camembert is a popular choice to take home and let sit until it is deliciously soft and runny.

For bread, one goes to the *boulangerie,* or bakery. The shopwindow and all the shelves are loaded with an awesome array of crusty loaves. There is the *baguette,* a long narrow loaf, and smaller loaves called *pain de mie,* or bakery bread. Alongside are Italian-style loaves. Then come breads made with walnuts, raisins, or anise; egg breads; and countless other varieties. The largest of all is the startling *pain de campagne,* or country bread, sometimes 3 feet long and a foot wide.

If Maman has taken the children shopping, they may feel there is still one more shop to visit: the *confiserie,* or candy shop. Boxes of delicious chocolates and hard candies are on display in the window, on the shelves, and on tables. Nearby are candied fruits in a profusion of choices: cherries dipped in white frosting, sugary pineapple segments, pears, dates, and apricots. It is almost impossible to make a decision—it all smells so good!

Stunning are the elegant food shops, such as the legendary Fauchon in Paris, in the Place de la Madeleine. Fauchon offers a wide range of exquisitely prepared foods for the réveillon table, including *terrines* (meat, fish, and game dishes served cold), pâtés, caviar, and fruits.

But now all is done, the shopping is finally completed. It is time to go home. Christmas Eve—and the réveillon—are fast approaching.

Flounder, turbot, sole, and prawns are among the choices offered at a poissonnerie, or fish shop, in Bayonne, on the southeastern coast of France.

The Château de Vizille Park lies covered by a dusting of snow in the French Alps.

Noëls from the Past

Christmas has been celebrated in France for more than 1,500 years. The religious observance is tied to important historical events. France was once part of an extensive region known as Gaul. The Romans conquered the area in the time of Julius Caesar, between 58 and 51 B.C, making Gaul a province of Rome. The Romans adopted Christianity in the 300's, and their legions carried it to Gaul.

In the 400's, a non-Christian German tribe called the Franks took over much of Gaul. By the end of the century, Clovis, the king of the Franks, was a powerful ruler. He married a Christian princess of Burgundy named Clotilda, who persuaded him to convert to her faith. On Christmas Day in 496, Saint Rémi, bishop of Reims, baptized Clovis and many of his warriors. And France's first Christmas celebration was observed.

The fabled warrior Charlemagne (Charles the Great) became king of the Franks in 768. In 799, Pope Leo III was driven from Rome after being accused of crimes against the church. Charlemagne granted him refuge and later presided

A statue of Charlemagne, king of the Franks, who was crowned emperor of the Romans on Christmas Day, 800, stands outside the Cathedral of Notre Dame in Paris.

over a tribunal in Rome in which the pope was proven innocent. On Christmas Day in the year 800, Pope Leo crowned Charlemagne emperor of the Romans. The splendid ceremony was held in the original Saint Peter's Church in Rome.

Christmas in the castle

Christmas in medieval France was a glorious occasion, especially at court. It was customary for the castle gates to remain open all through Christmas Night. Strangers were made welcome in the great dining halls, and no one ever asked the travelers' names or destinations.

If a needy guest appeared, the *châtelaine,* or lady of the castle, would slip a loaf of bread, a bit of meat, and perhaps a few coins into his pouch. Sometimes he might even go away the next day with a new coat, leaving his tattered old garment behind.

Christmas in the castles was a jolly, noisy affair, with hundreds of guests enjoying vast amounts of food—and quantities of wine and other spirits. Huge logs burned merrily in the tall fireplaces; torches cast their dim, smoky light upon the revelers. The chilly stone floors were strewn with rushes, herbs, and sweet-smelling grasses. Tapestries on the walls helped to keep out the drafts.

Fantastic banquets were served by hordes of scurrying servants. Peacock was a favorite dish, as were swan and even stork. In Charlemagne's day, the cooking was done over open fires. Fingers were usually the only utensils, except for a knife or dagger to cut the meat.

All sorts of entertainment accompanied the Christmas dinner: performances by jugglers, magicians, and dancers, and *masquerades* (stories told using masks and music). Outdoors there were often exciting jousting tournaments and wild boar hunts for the noble lords.

Although fun loving, the medieval French were at the same time pious. Kings and queens, lords and ladies, and the folk attended impressive Masses during the Christmas season. The lucky ones could enjoy services at one of the majestic new Gothic cathedrals such as Notre Dame in Chartres, which was constructed mainly during the 1200's.

Storytelling played an important role in the holiday celebrations, too, for both rich and poor. Traveling musicians sang and recited ancient legends in royal halls and in small villages to enthralled audiences. They often sang of miracles that took place on Christmas Eve.

Devotion to the real reason for Christmas—Christ's birth—was shown in medieval France in other ways besides churchgoing and storytelling. One custom came from Italy.

Saint Francis and the crèche

In 1223, Saint Francis re-created the event of Christ's birth with a live Nativity scene in the hills near Assisi, Italy. The beloved saint arranged a touching scene—a manger filled with hay, with a real ox and donkey to watch over the Newborn Child and breathe warmth upon Him.

Saint Francis placed a baby in the humble crib and then related the Nativity story to the villagers and shepherds who had gathered to witness the unusual event. The people loved the idea and, before long, the charming manger scene was being re-created in other villages throughout Italy. Somewhere along the way, a notion of also using miniature figures to tell the story was conceived.

From Italy, the custom spread to other European countries. There were both the live manger scenes and the ones with small replicas of Joseph, Mary, the Infant, and all the other Biblical characters. In time, new roles or figures, representing local people of diverse occupations, were added.

In France, the manger scene, or crèche, first appeared in Avignon sometime between 1316 and 1334. Legend says that members of Saint Francis's own family imported the tradition. The French people quickly adopted the idea, and over the years it became one of the more popular French Christmas customs. In Provence, artisans create the marvelous terra-cotta

Nobles feast at a banquet in a painting from an illuminated manuscript of the 1400's.

crèche figures called *santons*. The art form is unique to France, and the charming simplicity of the hand-painted figures is unmatched anywhere else in the world. Marseille is the home of the yearly santon fair, first held there in 1803.

The first Noël

Religious dramas called mystery or miracle plays also began to be performed in France during the Middle Ages. These plays were acted-out versions of the events surrounding Christ's life and the lives of the saints. Originally presented by the church, the dramas were devised to teach the Bible to the people, most of whom could not read or write. The earliest *noëls,* or French Christmas songs, appeared about that time, too.

An illuminated manuscript of the 1300's combines a painting of Christmas dancers with the notes and lyrics of an ancient noël, or Christmas song.

At first the noëls were hymns, solemn melodies sung in Latin. A new sort of noël began to be heard in the 1400's. This form was sung in local dialects, often to the tunes of popular songs. Noëls of this period sometimes contained nonreligious verses. The songs were included in the rural shepherds' plays, the pastorales. The noëls were sung both as key parts of the scenes and also as links from one scene to another.

The carols were so well liked that whole collections of them, called *bibles de noël,* were published between the 1500's and 1700's. By the beginning of the 1700's, French Christmas songs had become joyful and lively. In the 1800's, the noëls switched character once again and, reflecting the tone of the era, turned rather stiff and pompous.

Yet the most famous and beloved—though not most artistically admired—French noël of all was written during that period. It is the beautiful "Minuit, Chrétiens" or "Oh, Holy Night." The words to the carol, now sung all over the world, were written by Placide Cappeau, the mayor of the small town of Roquemaure.

Cappeau's business was selling wine, and as he traveled from village to village he would amuse himself by making up verses.

Children are dazzled by the delights of a fantasy toy palace in an engraving from the 1800's.

Onc day the curate of Roquemaure asked Monsieur Cappeau to write some verses for a Christmas carol. The curate wanted them for a member of his congregation, a Madame Laurcy, who had an especially fine voice.

On his next wine-selling journey, Monsieur Cappeau found the time to write the words to the poem he called "Minuit, Chrétiens." Madame Laurey liked the poem and took it to her friend, the celebrated composer Adolphe Adam. He was ill at the time and, to distract himself, composed a melody for Cappeau's poem.

Madame Laurey sang the carol for the first time during midnight Mass on Dec. 25, 1847, in the little church of Roquemaure. It was an instant success. Later, the noted baritone Jean-Baptiste Faure sang "Minuit, Chrétiens" at midnight Mass in a church in Paris, and the carol was on its way to worldwide fame. Today, all over France, church congregations traditionally sing the carol at the stroke of midnight on Christmas Eve.

The Holy Maiden intercedes on behalf of a child who has been naughty as Hans Trapp enters the room behind her in an Alsatian engraving from 1858.

The history of the tree

Although the custom of the Christmas tree does not go so far back in French history as many other Christmas traditions, there are mentions of Christmas trees beginning in the early 1600's. The area of their first appearance is Alsace-Lorraine, a historical province in the northeast of France, close to Germany.

The culture of the area once called Alsace-Lorraine has been part German and part French for hundreds of years. Both countries waged wars for control of the region, and though it has been French since 1945, German customs are still practiced by many of its people. Putting up a Christmas tree is one of the customs that began in Alsace-Lorraine and later spread westward.

In 1605, a traveler reported that the inhabitants of Strasbourg, on the German border, had fir trees in their homes at Christmas. The trees were, to his astonishment, adorned with paper roses, apples, candy, and sugary cookie wafers.

Paris was first introduced to the Christmas tree in 1837, when Princess Helen of Mecklenburg brought the charming notion with her to the city after her marriage to the Duke of Orléans. Refugees from Alsace-Lorraine popularized it when they settled in France after the Franco-Prussian War (1870-1871).

Hans Trapp and the Christ Child

Besides the Christmas tree, also from Alsace-Lorraine comes the legend of Hans Trapp and the young maiden, who represented the Christ Child. These two Christmas personalities were said to visit the children of Alsace-Lorraine on Christmas Eve.

The fearsome Hans Trapp was in charge of doling out punishment to those girls and boys who had not behaved well during the year. But the maiden interceded for the children. When they promised to behave better in the future, she led them to a Christmas tree loaded with presents, and their fear of Hans Trapp vanished.

A very old Christmas custom all over France was the burning of the yule log. A huge length of wood was cut and ceremoniously dragged into the house. The log was set aflame just as the family left for Christmas Eve services. In some areas, it was supposed to burn several hours, through the three consecutive Christmas Masses everyone had to attend. In other areas, attempts were made to keep the log burning even longer.

The yule log

The log was believed to have magical powers. A shepherdess might have tapped it with her crook to ensure a good lambing season. Even the log's embers were magical—the more sparks they sent out, the better the harvest was going to be. No one ever dared sit on the log as it was being prepared for the hearth, of course. If someone did, it was believed he or she would be cursed with an attack of *boils* (areas of painful, red swelling on the skin) within two days.

Many homes nowadays do not have fireplaces, and the old-time custom of the yule log has for the most part disappeared in France. It is not forgotten, though. The bûche de Noël, the Christmas cake shaped like a yule log and covered with chocolate "bark," appears in bakeshops and homes throughout France each Christmas.

A father blesses the yule log on Christmas Eve as his family gathers round, in an Alsatian engraving from the 1800's.

Christmas light sculptures frame the Sacre-Coeur basilica in Montmartre, a neighborhood on a hill overlooking Paris.

Christmas Eve in Paris

Christmas Eve has come, and the beautiful city of Paris is alight. Along the Champs-Élysées, toward the Arc de Triomphe, tree branches are strung with white lights. The arches of the Pont des Invalides are curves of light, reflecting like silvery garlands in the black waters below. Fir trees at the base of the Eiffel Tower are adorned with lights and garlands, too.

There is an air of excitement everywhere as shoppers make last-minute purchases of gifts and food before going home. This is a very special night for the children of Paris. Soon, Père Noël will come, bringing gifts to place in the children's shoes.

Petit Jésus, or Little Jesus, once was believed to visit the children personally on Christmas Night. Later, in many parts of the country, the Christmas spirit was called Petit Noël, or Little Christmas. Today, most French children believe Jesus sends Père Noël, or Father Christmas, in His place.

A visit by Père Noël

Père Noël does not look like the American Santa Claus; he is not a plump little man who comes riding in a sleigh drawn by reindeer. Instead, he is tall and slender, an imposing old man with a white beard, wearing a long red robe edged with fur. Sometimes he wears wooden shoes. He carries a sackful of toys and goodies, and a donkey often accompanies him to help with the heavy sack. Père Noël does not say "Ho, ho, ho!" as Santa Claus does, either. He may wish children "Joyeux Noël" (Merry Christmas).

On Christmas Eve, French children place their shoes, slippers, or boots near the fireplace, if there is one. If not, the shoes are set near the Christmas tree or the crèche. Sometimes the youngsters are allowed to use Papa's shoes—or big brother's—because the footwear is so much larger and can hold more presents.

And, now and then, in the true spirit of Christmas, a family will arrange for other children from the neighborhood to place their shoes at the family hearth. Père Noël's generosity does not become strained during the Christmas Eve rush.

Père Noël has an entire country to visit on Christmas Eve, and he gets a bit hungry during his travels. So, children often leave a little snack for him, and sometimes even a glass of wine. Thoughtful youngsters will also leave a bit of food for the donkey.

A child places her slippers at the hearth in hopes that Père Noël will fill them with toys and sweets.

Late Christmas Eve, Père Noël will come, walking with his donkey. He will leave the animal outside the house and then come down the chimney. If there is no chimney, no matter; he will get in somehow—for Père Noël is magical.

As the children wait for Père Noël, Maman is finishing up her last-minute preparations for the réveillon to take place after midnight Mass. Usually a light snack of some sort is served before going to church because it will be a long time until the family returns for the big Christmas meal.

Older children or adults may tell Christmas stories to the little ones at this time, filling their minds with the wonder and merriment of the season.

The story of the three Masses

The most famous French Christmas story—and the one most beloved by the people of France—was published by Alphonse Daudet in 1875. Its title is "The Three Low Masses." (A low Mass is a simple one, celebrated without music; it was the most common type of Mass before 1969.)

Daudet is said to be the French Charles Dickens. And the story of the three Masses is, at least in popularity, the French counterpart to *A Christmas Carol,* Dickens's story abut Tiny Tim and the miser Ebenezer Scrooge.

But "The Three Low Masses" is unlike Dickens's story because it is not about someone who loves money. Instead, it is about people who love food. They love food so much, in fact, that on Christmas Eve they forget their devotion to God. Their punishment is a heavy one, and one that makes French children listening to the story think twice before misbehaving in any way on holy Christmas Night.

The story has a historical basis. For many hundreds of years, three consecutive Masses were celebrated on Christmas Eve in the churches and cathedrals of France. The worshipers became so hungry from having to sit through so many hours of devotions that, when they arrived home, they were famished. That was how the réveillon began: everyone was in the mood for a tremendous meal after Mass. And sometimes they were ready for it even before the Masses began.

According to Daudet, such was the state of Father Balaguère one Christmas Eve, just before midnight, when he was speaking to his altar boy, Garrigou:

"Two turkeys, Garrigou?" he asked.

"Yes, Your Reverence," the boy replied. "Two magnificent turkeys. They're so fat, their skin is stretched to groaning. And there are many other good things, too: plump, juicy trout, and quail and wine, and …"

"Enough, Garrigou!" the priest stopped the boy. "Quickly, help me dress for the services. For it is Christmas Eve, and we must not think only of food. Light the candles and ring the bell for the start of the first Mass. Hurry!"

In the 1870's, Alphonse Daudet wrote one of France's best-loved Christmas stories, "The Three Low Masses."

In truth, Garrigou the altar boy was not what he seemed. The Devil, on this night, had crept into the boy to lure Father Balaguère into the sin of gluttony, or greedy eating. And, even as the Mass began, the good priest's thoughts were on Garrigou's descriptions of the food to come, not on the prayers of the Mass.

Garrigou rang his little bell, a tinkly sound. To Father Balaguère it seemed as though the bell was speaking. "Let's get going," it seemed to say. "The sooner we finish, the sooner we'll get to eat!"

That time and every time the bell rang afterward, the good priest forgot the Mass. He thought of the kitchen, the platters of food—those turkeys with their stuffing—oh, delight!

... on Christmas Eve the old chapel ... seems to come to life once again ...

Somehow he managed to get through the first Mass, and he started on the second. The bell rang: "Ting-a-ling-ling, ting-a-ling-ling!" To Father Balaguère it said, "Quick, quick, let's get going!" And this time the priest raced through the Mass, speaking as rapidly as he possibly could. Garrigou (still with the Devil inside him) jabbered away just as fast with his responses at the altar.

"Two down!" the priest sighed as the second Mass came to an end. And without taking a breath he plunged into the third Mass.

"Ting-a-ling-ling, ting-a-ling-ling," the bell rang again. Father Balaguère was lost. He skipped some verses, he did not finish others, and he completely forgot the Lord's Prayer. He simply hurled himself through the final Mass.

The congregation was startled at first and a bit frightened. What was wrong with Father Balaguère? Some of the people stood when they should have been kneeling; others knelt when they should have been standing. The Mass was turning into total confusion. But no one objected; the congregation wanted to go home for the réveillon, too.

Quickly the third Mass came to an end, and Father Balaguère wasted no time reaching the dining room. And he ate. And he ate. And ate. He ate so much that, during the night, he suffered a dreadful attack of indigestion and died.

The next morning Father Balaguère arrived in heaven. God was exceedingly angry and said: "You stole the Christmas Masses from Me, and you will pay 300 times for your sin. You will not be allowed to enter paradise until you have celebrated 300 full Christmas Eve Masses in your own chapel. And that goes for all your congregation, who sinned with you."

So, the story goes, on Christmas Eve the old chapel of Father Balaguère—lying now in ruins on the lands of Trinquilage—seems to come to life once again. Mysterious candles flicker, and the murmurs of distant voices may be heard. Some people believe that Father Balaguère himself, Garrigou, and the entire congregation are celebrating the Christmas Masses. And, perhaps, getting close to number 300!

Attending midnight Mass

Maman has finished her preparations. Now comes the moment the youngsters have been waiting for ever since they helped set up the crèche a few days before. It is time to place Little Jesus in His crib. The moment is very solemn.

Maman hands the tiny image to one of the children, perhaps the youngest, who very carefully takes it and approaches the crèche. Gently the Infant is laid into the miniature manger. The figures of Mary and Joseph look on with pride, and the Three Wise Men, all the shepherds, angels, and other figures do, too. The children say a little prayer to the newly born Christ Child to complete the ceremony.

Although older French children often accompany their parents to midnight

A Christmas tree sparkles in front of Paris's Cathedral of Notre Dame, which is packed with worshipers during midnight Mass every year.

Mass, the younger ones usually do not. They are tucked into bed to dream like youngsters everywhere of the presents to come in the morning. As soon as the children are safely asleep, Maman and Papa add the final touches to the Christmas tree: candies, fruit, and small toys snuggled into the branches. Then it is time to set off for church.

People of many faiths attend the Catholic Masses held in France's beautiful cathedrals and churches, some of which are several hundred years old. The glorious midnight Masses are more than just church services—they are cultural events.

There are more than 200 churches in Paris alone. Many, including the Church of Saint-Eustache and the Cathedral of Notre Dame, are renowned for their splendid Christmas Eve music. At Notre Dame the crowds are enormous, and the traffic around the cathedral virtually comes to a halt around the time of the Mass.

One year, the traffic was so tangled at Notre Dame that a cardinal, not wishing to be late in arriving for midnight Mass, left his limousine where it was trapped in a solid line of cars and walked the rest of the way. As he reached the cathedral, some

Incense clouds the air as people of many faiths gather in Notre Dame, drawn by the cathedral's choirs and organ music.

children waiting in the crowd saw his red garb and thought he was Père Noël. The cardinal's entry into the cathedral was delayed for several more minutes, while he explained his true identity.

Inside, magnificent Notre Dame is packed with people every year. Most are wearing somber clothing of blues and browns; the priests are all in white.

The Mass is celebrated under the cathedral's massive Gothic arches, which were constructed beginning in 1163. Simple flower arrangements decorate the altars. Wisps of smoke curl up from the many, many flickering candles. Music from the mighty organ swells and ebbs, and the people of Paris lift their voices in song.

A symphony accompanies the soloist and choir during a traditional Christmas Eve noël at L'église Saint-Eustache, a church in Paris's Les Halles area.

Saint-Eustache lures Parisians with its symphony and choirs of both adults and children. And some Parisians at Christmastime will make a traditional pilgrimage all the way to Chartres, known as France's Christmas cathedral, perhaps to hear the beautiful voices of a special group called the Petits chanteurs de la croix de bois, or the little singers of the wooden cross. They are the French counterpart of the Vienna Boys' Choir.

At the conclusion of the Mass the bells ring out, and Christmas is joyously welcomed in. Heading home, the people can see the Eiffel Tower shining forth, a Christmas tree of white lights almost a thousand feet tall. The moment of the réveillon has come.

Finally, réveillon

Réveillon means "awakening." The Christmas Eve meal is enjoyed with all the gusto of New Year's Eve in the United States. Restaurants in Paris remain open on Christmas Eve, for some people prefer to dine out this night. Most, however, make their way home from Mass for their own private réveillon. Families invite relatives

A family gathers around the table for the highlight of the evening, an elaborate réveillon.

and friends to share the Christmas meal; often large numbers of guests accept the invitation. And the réveillon can last all night.

The meal is tackled with high spirits and a sharp appetite. It is a happy, warm time of sharing, enjoying marvelous foods, and offering countless toasts with France's fine wines. The table is set with candles and a lovely cloth, perhaps an heirloom of Breton or Alençon lace.

Throughout the lengthy meal, the hosts barely have time to sit or eat, as they prepare and serve course after course. And there may be as many as 15 courses! However, serving the réveillon is a labor of love.

There is also the wine. Many different kinds may be served, and they must first be tasted. It is always possible that a bottle will come from a bad batch or that the wine will have turned to vinegar. The host uncorks the bottle with great ceremony, sniffs the cork, pours a bit of wine into his own glass, and tastes it. If all is well, then and only then will he fill his guests' glasses.

In Paris, the réveillon frequently begins with delectable oysters on the half shell. Then may come canapés and hors d'oeuvres, plus *pâté de foie gras,* or goose liver pâté—a favorite among many French families. A plump, golden-brown turkey could follow, or perhaps a goose stuffed with prunes and pâté. Whatever the bird, it is surrounded by all the trimmings: potatoes, peas, salad. No family favorite is left out.

Later there will be cheeses—perhaps Camembert, Brie, and Boursin. The more kinds, the better. And bread with sweet butter is always served in great quantity. Fruit is never left out, and neither are nuts: walnuts, pecans—all kinds. And, finally comes the special Christmas cake: the rich, delicious bûche de Noël.

Each course may be accompanied by an appropriate wine, but some families provide a special treat: champagne, all the way through. At last, coffee is served, plus brandy and other liqueurs.

At this point, some families will open their presents. But parents with little children try to sneak in a few hours' sleep towards dawn on Christmas morning. They need it—for when the little ones emerge, sleepy-eyed and tousled, they are in a great state of excitement. Père Noël has come!

Christmas morning

The shoes left empty the night before are now hidden beneath piles of brightly wrapped gifts. And the snack for Père Noël is gone. Only a few crumbs remain. His glass of wine is empty, too. Even the treat left for the donkey has disappeared, to the youngsters' great joy.

Maman and Papa, worn out from the réveillon, sip coffee and watch while the children tear open their presents: dolls, trucks, or

Children delight in the gifts Père Noël has left under the family tree.

racing cars, a stuffed animal or two, compact discs, books and games. And sweets—perhaps a chocolate wooden shoe or Père Noël.

The grown-ups' celebration is yet to come. They will exchange their gifts on New Year's Day. But for the youngsters, Christmas is the big day, indeed. Père Noël has read their letters carefully. Somehow—with the help of loving parents?—he has managed to bring exactly the right gifts. The children of Paris have had a glorious Noël.

A cottage lies nestled in the trees above a ski slope in the Savoy region of the French Alps.

Noël in the Provinces

Hundreds of years ago, France was made up of provinces ruled by kings, princes, and lesser nobility. In the 1700's, the people overthrew the despised Bourbon monarchy during the French Revolution. The provinces were abolished in 1790, and a new constitution was signed in 1791. The country was then divided into departments, each named for a mountain or stream.

More than 200 years have passed since the change from historical provinces to modern departments was made. Yet, even today citizens of Nice, in the province of Provence, think of themselves as Provençals rather than as belonging to the department of the Maritime Alps. The old ways are still cherished—especially the old ways of celebrating Christmas.

Over the centuries, French Christmas celebrations have become an intricately woven tapestry of customs. Many regions share the same traditions; others have developed distinctly different ones. And some regions share their customs with Germany, Spain, and Italy—three countries that border France.

The Christmas climate varies, too, from the crisp, cold air and snow-clad slopes of the mountain regions to the semitropical warmth of the Mediterranean coast. In between are more temperate areas: rolling plains, a great central plateau, and the fertile valleys where grapes for French wines are grown.

Christmas in the French Alps

Many French families spend at least part of the Christmas holidays skiing, so ski resorts do a brisk business at this time of year. The French Alps are especially popular for winter vacationing. Even the younger members of the family sweep happily down the steep slopes, sometimes taking a tumble into the soft drifts.

It is also fun to take a sleigh ride. The horses' hoofs squeak on the packed snow as they trot along narrow streets or head out into open countryside. The runners glide so effortlessly, it feels as though the sleigh is flying. The air is nippy cold, but everyone is bundled up in warm coats and scarves. Children's cheeks burn rosy red; their eyes sparkle with pleasure. Even the horses seem to enjoy the trip, snorting clouds of steamy breath as they prance along, sleigh bells jingling.

The alpine scene is picture-perfect. Snowflakes drift lazily through the air. The branches of fir trees droop with their white burden. In the background and all around are massive mountains covered in deep, deep layers of snow and ice.

The small mountain villages look like classic scenes from Christmas cards. In the town square, a tall tree may stand, aglitter with lights and ornaments. More holiday decorations hang suspended on wires over the village streets. And many homes have their own Christmas tree. Shiny green branches of red-berried holly are visible through the windows, and usually some mistletoe, too. At night the stars twinkle frostily in the blue-black sky. Rustic chapels, all alight, cast a glow of golden warmth across the snow.

An antique sleigh carries holiday visitors through the snow-covered countryside of the French Alps.

The historic province of Dauphiné in the French Alps is a cold, almost bleak mountain region. Icy ridges stretch for almost 100 square miles (260 square kilometers). Hidden valleys lie below, shadowed by the snowbound crests. The tops of these mountains are capped with snow the year around.

Bustling ski resorts have sprung up in the French Alps in recent years. But some parts of Dauphiné are still very isolated during the winter. Sometimes so much snow falls that it forms a vault between the roofs of the houses. The people of one mountain range, the Oisans, share a special kind of kinship that comes from battling the elements together, year after year.

A villager in the Alps decorates the window of her home with holly.

Life in the villages of the Oisans range has always been difficult, but the hardships have eased in modern times. Nowadays, most houses have central heating systems. At one time, however, heating supplies were so precious that a whole village would gather in a single stable for warmth and light in the evenings. This custom was born of necessity, and it was one that also brought entire communities—animals included—together for such feasts as the réveillon.

Christmas Eve has always been a special time for the people of the Oisans range. Even the animals in the stables receive extra food as a holiday treat. According to one ancient legend, the animals kneel at the stroke of midnight in honor of the Infant Jesus. Another says that the statues of the saints in the chapels leave their niches at midnight on Christmas Eve to worship the Christ Child at the crèche.

In winter, light takes on a special meaning in this mountain region. The days are so short, and the nights so very long. Springtime seems far away. In some villages, the sun disappears completely for several months, hidden by the towering mountain

Foods from the réveillon are placed in a stable in the mountainous Oisans region on Christmas Eve, with the hope that angels will come to share the feast.

peaks. Only a grayish gloom remains to light the steps of the villagers.

In earlier times, people were not always certain that spring—and the shining sun—would ever return. So, they lighted great bonfires called "fires of joy" as celebrations of hope. Even today, in some communities, a modern Christmas custom honors the power of light. Skiers holding torches weave their way down the steep slopes, making a brilliant pattern of light against the darkness.

In many villages, the townsfolk light up the night of Christmas Eve with lanterns. Streets are dotted with small, moving lights as people hurry to the chapels for midnight Mass. The services are simple and solemn, with flickering candles and traditional carols.

Midnight comes, and with it, Christmas in the Alps. After Mass, the villagers head homeward through the silent night. "Noël, Noël!" they call to one another as the church bells echo the sound. It is time for the réveillon, the Christmas feast.

A simpler réveillon

In this frozen region, the foods are plain—not at all like the fancy fare of Paris and other large cities. The meal starts with a large bowl of hot soup, much appreciated after the walk through the cold outdoors. The soup is a bouillon, or clear broth, with *luzans,* a kind of pasta cut into diamond shapes. Then come *ravioles,* or stuffed pasta squares.

The main course may be a platter of boiled beef, or an omelet served with *escargots,* or snails. Even the omelet was once a traditional offering to the sun, in hopes the sun would soon reappear. For dessert, there is an enormous tart, a delicious pie filled with prunes, pears, or squash.

In the old days, when the réveillon was held in the stable, the tablecloth would be carefully folded up over any remaining food and left there. Then, it was said, the Christmas angels coming to visit would be able to enjoy a Christmas snack themselves.

New Year's Day had its traditions, too, in the Alps. Housewives saved their best flour to make a loaf of white bread, the only one of the year and considered a great treat. The loaf was called the *chalanda*. And branches of juniper were burned in front of the houses to ensure prosperity in the coming year.

A blend of traditions

In southern France, near Spain, the people of Perpignan observe a mixture of both French and Spanish traditions. They speak Catalan, the local dialect. Here in the Pyrenees mountains, children eagerly await their presents on January 6, not on Christmas Day. And the gifts are brought not by Père Noël but by the Three Wise Men.

La Rochelle, on the Atlantic coast, is an old, historical port city, far away from the mountain peaks. Cobblestone streets, medieval towers, and fishing boats create the backdrop for Noël by the sea.

In December, a click-clack, click-clack is mixed with the sounds coming from the docks. For, at Christmastime, La Rochelle turns its streets festive with a live Père Noël, dressed in his red robe and sporting wooden shoes.

The Père Noël of La Rochelle is a merry, white-bearded sign of Christmas. His gifts are hidden not in a sack, but in a basket strapped to his back. He tempts children of all ages to come see what Christmas joy he has brought with him to the seaside.

Farther to the north, this time on the English Channel, is Mont-Saint-Michel. It is a large rock that juts from the foggy waters of Mont-Saint-Michel Bay, in Normandy. At the top of the rock are a medieval abbey and town.

The abbey of Mont-Saint-Michel is the site of Christmas pilgrimages. Hardy Normans and not-so-hardy tourists wishing to

Skiers at d'Auris-Station in the Oisans mountain range welcome the birth of Christ with a torchlight procession (top). A tree lights the way to a rustic chapel in Méribel for midnight Mass (above).

A Provençal Christmas dance re-creates the joy of angels and shepherds when Christ was born.

attend Mass there follow the priests and dignitaries up the winding streets of the town, then up hundreds of stairs, until they finally reach the abbey.

After services in nearby Brittany, Bretons may sit down to a traditional réveillon of buckwheat cakes and rich cream. The talk will likely be about the sea at one point or another, for there are many fine seaports with deep harbors in Brittany. Many Bretons become sailors or fishermen, and a rich folklore has developed about the sea. One popular story tells about the *ange de la mer,* the angel of the sea, who appears each Christmas Eve. A great white wing with feathers edged in black represents the angel. The wing guides ships lost at sea to safety on Christmas Night.

A Provençal Christmas

With all respect for the rest of France, the people of Provence, in the southeast, claim that nowhere else in the country is Christmas more devoutly observed. Certainly the Provençals celebrate the season with a great deal of exuberance. They have been enjoying Christmas in their own special way for centuries.

Provence's climate and its rugged terrain are somewhat similar to those of ancient Judea. Centuries ago, some inhabitants of the region believed that Jesus was really born in Provence, not in faraway Bethlehem, and that Provençal shepherds were the first to hear the news of Christ's birth.

Provence has its own Christmas dance, called the *farandole*. Legend has it that, after hearing the news that Christ was born, the shepherds, shepherdesses, and townspeople of Provence made up the dance on the way to see the Holy Child—in Bethlehem-en-Provence, of course.

Provence, however, is not the only area of France that has claimed to be the birthplace of the Holy Child. Auvergne, in the mountains of south-central France, and also Brittany are two other regions with the same legend.

Still, the splendor of Christmas in Provence is hard to match. One knows the joyful season is coming when community groups begin to present Provençal carols at community gatherings. The singers wear native costumes dating back centuries.

During the Middle Ages, the people in this region began a custom that has lost none of its popularity. On Christmas Eve, many Provençal villages reenact the story of the Nativity with a grand procession of shepherds and pilgrims. Frequently the procession ends with a living crèche.

The tradition probably began as a pageant staged in a local castle, acted out by the noble lords and ladies to entertain their guests. In later years, the townspeople adopted the custom for themselves, in a simpler, more meaningful way.

Near the ancient town of Les Baux, the annual procession moves toward the tiny church of Saint Vincent, founded in the Middle Ages. Les Baux is situated on a craggy, windswept plateau high above flat marshes. There are only a few hundred villagers in Les Baux, living among the ruins of a medieval fortress and town that flourished in the Middle Ages. The community of several thousand people was repeatedly devastated by wars. Today, it is a destination for tourists, with the remains of its castle looming precariously over the ruins.

At night, when the ruins are floodlighted, it is easy to imagine the castle as it once was. The

Real animals join a living crèche in an enactment of the Nativity scene in the town of Les Baux in Provence.

Fishing boats sparkle with holiday lights on a river near Laval in northwestern France.

visitor can almost see grand entourages of kings and popes, or knights in silvery armor clattering their way along the cobbled streets.

The story of Les Baux

The story of Les Baux began with a legendary ruler named Balthasar. He, it is said, was descended from the legendary King Balthasar, who was one of the Three Wise Men. Balthasar came to the area at the time of the Roman occupation. His descendants built their massive fortress on a table of rock that they named Les Baux, after the Provençal word *baou,* or rocky slope.

The coat of arms the feudal lords adopted is embellished with a 16-rayed star. The people of Les Baux call it the Christmas Star, the star that led King Balthasar and his companions to the Christ Child.

The lords of Les Baux were mighty and very proud during medieval times. Their fortress was the seat of one of the more powerful ancient feudal houses in Provence. These nobles were masters of many towns and villages between the Alps and the sea.

In 1632, King Louis XIII and Cardinal Richelieu ordered the destruction of the castle to diminish the power of the feudal lords. The area was given to the Grimaldi family, rulers of Monaco, whose land it has remained ever since. The new rulers partially rebuilt the fortress over the years, but during the French Revolution it was gutted by fire.

In later years the village on the rock became a haven for artists and writers, and the villagers became known for their fine handcrafted woodcarvings, pottery, and jewelry. And Les Baux became well known for its Christmas Eve procession, called the "Fête de pâstrage."

The Christmas Eve procession

The procession begins about an hour before midnight. Hundreds of participants wait patiently for the signal to light their candles. Then, like a curving ribbon of flame in the darkness, the figures slowly make their way toward the church.

All the characters of the original Nativity story are there—Joseph and Mary, angels of all sizes, the Three Kings, attired in gorgeous robes, and a host of shepherds and shepherdesses, all wearing their traditional brown woolen cloaks. Behind them come pilgrims from throughout the area, dressed in colorful regional costumes.

The ceremony begins as the procession enters the church. The choir softly sings an old Provençal carol, accompanied by shepherds playing *galoubets,* or fifes, and *tambourins,* the long, narrow drums of the region. Joseph, Mary, and the angels take their places at a living crèche set in a tiny chapel near the altar. The rest of the procession waits.

The priest appears and the Mass begins. At the Offertory—the part of the Mass when the parishioners bring the wine and the bread to the altar—the chief shepherd makes his way up the aisle. He leads a handsome, beribboned ram. It is pulling a small wooden cart, decorated with greenery, ribbons, and lighted candles. Inside the cart, a tiny lamb lies on a soft bed of moss.

Mary hands the priest a wax image of Little Jesus, and the priest holds the Infant high to show the congregation. Then the priest sits, still holding the Child, as the shepherds come one by one to bow and kiss the feet of the little image.

The lead shepherd now picks up the lamb and offers him to Jesus.

Villagers dressed in regional costumes join a traditional Christmas Eve procession in Les Baux in Provence.

The Three Kings move forward to present their gifts, too. And the shepherds come, each with a simple gift of honey or cheese, a live piglet, or a soft toy lamb. The Mass continues.

Just at the moment when the priest lifts the Host and chalice and the altar boys ring their tinkly bells, a shepherd tweaks the lamb's tail. It bleats, just like the cries of the Christ Child.

The drums roll—it is midnight! The choir and congregation joyously sing "Minuit, Chrétiens," "Oh, Holy Night." The lamb is passed from shepherd to shepherd. Each one in turn bows to the Christ Child. Finally, the Mass ends, and the church empties to the cries of "Joyeux Noël!"

The Provençal town of Séguret also has a spectacular Christmas Eve procession, this time to the church of Saint-Denis. A huge, brilliant star is placed each year on a crag overlooking the village, to lead pilgrims from afar. The ceremony is called the "Bergie de Séguret," and the townspeople rehearse their roles for months in advance.

An organist in the church of Solliès-Ville plays the oldest organ in France, dating to 1499, during midnight Mass on Christmas Eve.

Provençal traditions

In Solliès-Ville, another small town of Provence, the Christmas Eve celebration begins with an unusual ceremony. The entire village gathers at the town hall, where the mayor, imposing in his tricolored sash, makes a speech. Twelve village children stand waiting across a table. They are dressed in white vestments and represent the 12 apostles. When the mayor's speech is done, he hands each child a small gift, called an *obole*.

The custom began many years ago, when two local brothers distributed flour to all the town's needy at Christmastime. Now the gifts are presented to children. And instead of bread, the oboles are much more appealing: chocolate bars and fruit, for instance. Real loaves of bread are handed out to the audience, however, preserving the tradition in full. Later, the town's dignitaries hold a festive supper.

On arriving at the church in Solliès-Ville, parishioners find a living crèche, with children representing the manger figures. This crèche has a special feature: a live baby plays the part of Little Jesus. The custom of having a live Christ Child for the crèche was once fairly widespread in Provence. In recent times, however, fewer towns keep the tradition.

Solliès-Ville has another important token from the past, one that fills its church with Christmas gladness each year. The organ in the church of Solliès-Ville is one of the oldest in France, dating from 1499. The antique instrument has provided music for midnight Mass for more than 500 years.

Réveillon in Provence may begin with a clear broth, often of pheasant. Roast pheasant may appear as the main course, too, as may lamb, wrapped in a crust. But when one thinks of réveillon in Provence, the dish that springs to mind first is lobster—piles of the delicious shellfish, boiled to sweet perfection.

Served along with crusty loaves of bread are green salads, cheeses, pâtés, and several wines. And, not one—but 13—desserts. The 13 desserts are an ancient custom, symbolizing Christ and the 12 apostles. Sometimes the delicacies are served heaped in glazed pottery bowls. Families also present the desserts more formally, carefully arranged on silver platters that grace the buffet.

A Provence réveillon often features pheasant and turkey as well as fish and especially oysters and lobster. Grand-mére has prepared the 13 desserts of réveillon for her family (bottom).

A pastry maker offers a bûche de Noël that is the size of a real log.

There might be marzipan, nuts of all kinds, dark and light nougat, dried figs and dates, preserves, glazed fruit, and fresh fruit—oranges, winter pears, grapes, and apples. And cakes—a favorite is the *galette de Noël,* which is a flat, deep-fried disk dusted with sugar and dipped into warm honey. Another possibility is the *fougasse,* a sweet, buttery bread with cinnamon and sometimes anise. The fougasse is also served at Epiphany by some families.

A Provençal specialty is called *panado.* This Christmas tart filled with apples may be set among the 13 desserts as a special treat.

The yule log

The yule log tradition was once popular in many areas of France, including Provence. The custom may have developed from a medieval feudal tax called the "right of the log." Each Christmas Eve the peasants had to bring a mighty length of wood from the forest to the feudal lord's manor. Eventually, the people began ceremoniously bringing logs into their own homes at Christmas. Great ceremonies developed around how the log was to be blessed and how it was to be lighted.

In Provence, the lighting of the fire was called *cacho fio.* A yule log, often with the charred remains of the last Christmas Eve log, was laid on the hearth and set aflame. Everyone in the household gathered around to watch the ceremony, each with a glass of wine. The youngest member of the family dipped a twig into his or her glass and tossed the twig into the fire. The oldest, probably Grand-père, then hurled his glass into the flames as he recited a prayer. In one form or other, this prayer existed in most French provinces.

In Brittany, custom required that the eldest and youngest members of the family light the fire together. Then they offered the traditional prayer to Little Jesus. The Breton version of the blessing goes like this:

Christmas log, catch fire
Let us all rejoice.
Lord, give us Thy peace

And pour over us Thy blessing.
Lord, let us also
See the coming year.
And, if we are not one more,
May we not be one less.

The yule log was once an important Christmas tradition in Burgundy, too. In one town, a local castle supposedly had a log so large, a horse had to drag it through the great front door and all the way to the massive fireplace in the dining hall.

Before being put into the hearth, the yule log was sometimes used as a hiding place. On Christmas Eve, Burgundian fathers would tuck some goodies underneath the log: nuts, dried fruits, perhaps a coin. The children would go into another room to say their prayers to the Christ Child. They would come back when Papa called them and strike the log with a stick to make it give up what was "in its stomach." Then the children would search for the goodies.

Sometimes, Papa would tease the youngsters and put nothing at all under the log. He would tell the disappointed youngsters

A tree farmer in Burgundy packs spruce trees for shipment throughout France.

that they had not hit the log hard enough. Back to the other room they would go, to pray a little longer. Eventually, of course, Papa rewarded their efforts— or was it Little Jesus?

The yule log was a magical object, in Burgundy and other areas. One could gauge the harvest to come by striking the log's embers with tongs: the more the log crackled with sparks, the more sheafs of corn there would be. Once burned, the remaining cinders had medicinal powers. Put into the soil, they

could prevent grain diseases. During storms, one had only to throw a handful of cinders into the hearth to keep lightning away from the house.

Special traditions of Burgundy

Besides the yule log, one of the more widespread traditions in Burgundy was the "singing quest," which took place on Christmas Eve, before the log was placed in the hearth. Youngsters ran through the streets of towns and villages carrying lighted candles and singing carols. They would stop at every shop—the butcher's, the baker's, the grocer's—to beg for treats. The children continued their quest until their candles were burned down to the nubs. This search was supposed to commemorate Joseph and Mary's journey from house to house, seeking lodging on the Holy Night.

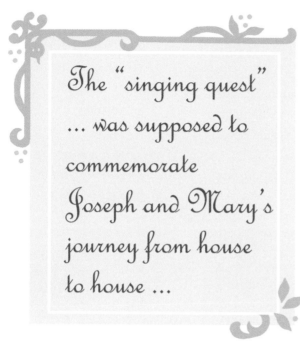

The "singing quest" ... was supposed to commemorate Joseph and Mary's journey from house to house ...

Another Burgundian custom was especially picturesque. Children in some towns made small sacks from paper. Inside, they would tuck a coin. On Christmas Eve, the youngsters stood in their windows and tossed the sacks into the dark streets, first lighting one corner of the bag. Those in need could easily find the gifts, guided by the lights—like tiny shooting stars.

The Burgundians cherished the Christmas holiday so much that the name of the Christmas season itself was used as a year-round cheer. People cried "Noël, Noël!" to greet passing nobility or other distinguished persons. The greeting was also commonly used for almost every special occasion—at marriages, births, even the signing of peace treaties.

Midnight Mass

In France, almost everyone attends one of the midnight Masses on Christmas Eve. The services range from grandly impressive ones in mighty cathedrals, where choirs sing accompanied by the deep tones of ancient organs, to simple observances in village churches.

In the extreme northeast of Alsace, on the German border, Mass is celebrated in a historic convent church high on the

mountain of Sainte-Odile, above Strasbourg and the Rhine River. On Christmas Eve, the beautiful old church is illuminated. Its light shines for miles, into the countryside of both Germany and France.

South of Paris, in the Loire Valley, visitors are invited to hear magnificent Gregorian chants sung at the 1,000-year-old Benedictine abbey church at Saint-Benoît-sur-Loire and at the Benedictine abbey in Solesmes, founded in 1010.

On the island of Corsica, in the Mediterranean Sea, the capital of Ajaccio offers a completely different type of Christmas music. There, churches ring with ancient Corsican carols, showing the influence of Italy, which once ruled the island.

At the church of Saint-Benoît of the Cap-d'Antibes, in Provence, worshipers are invited to see a European crèche made with characters representing all the countries of medieval Europe. And nearby, at La Colle-sur-Loup, the faithful may observe a Tahitian Noël.

To make sure absolutely no one is left out, the airport in Nice provides Mass in the terminal for travelers unlucky enough to be away from home on the Holy Night.

Children dressed as figures in a Nativity scene gather around the altar during Christmas Eve Mass in Provence.

Services are advertised all over the country: in the newspapers, on television and radio, over the Internet, and on posters or fliers, which are popular French vehicles for announcing events. A few posters even include a poetic touch and a timely message to the reader. This one is for the Christmas Eve services at the church of Saint-Antoine Ginestière, in Nice:

Noël, for some, is pleasure, parties, the réveillon, skiing. Let us not permit these pleasures to make us thoughtless. The "alarm bells" ring out at Christmas to alert our hearts: Let us share the sufferings of those sick, alone, at war. But let us also share our joys with them. Then, the true joy of Christmas is in us.

The announcement continues:

We suggest that you come to express this joy by joining our chorale, which, after 11 o'clock tonight, will begin the Christmas Eve service. Then, by the light of candles, "Oh, Holy Night" will arise, demonstrating the intense emotions of our souls. After will come the moment of meditation: the midnight Mass, where each, in communion with all, will pray according to his own heart. Come find the joy that Jesus offers you and celebrate with us the coming to earth of the Son of God.

The poster's message concludes with one final, practical note:

Paix et joie! Parking spacieux et gratuit.
Peace and joy! Spacious, free parking lot.

Especially in the cities of France, many of the old ways of observing Christmas threaten to disappear. Much of the countryside, however, still clings to ancient rituals and pageantry. The carolers, the pastorales, the living crèches, the pilgrimages, the traditional réveillon foods—all combine to create a holiday that hearkens back to celebrations many hundreds of years in the past.

Everywhere, churches overflow with worshipers on Christmas Eve. Families gather later, sharing the Holy Night. The customs are beautiful, all blending together to create the joyous celebration called Noël.

A family crèche occupies a place of honor beneath the Christmas tree in a home in Alsace.

The Santons of Provence

At the heart of Noël throughout all of France are tiny clay figures known as santons. They originated in the province of Provence. In fact, "santon" comes from the word "santoùon," which means "little saint" in the Provençal dialect. The figurines may be hand-painted or clothed, and they are used to depict the Nativity scene. However, instead of the traditional characters of Bethlehem and the Holy Land, santons reflect people from Provençal village life of the 1700's and 1800's as they visit the Christ Child and bring Him gifts. The simplicity of these manger figures, the rural charm of their humble dress, and their incredible variety are unique.

A scene from traditional French village life is re-created with a collection of santons, or "little saints."

All the characters of the old French countryside are found among the "little saints." Placed in the crèche, they resemble real people, in the detail of their expressions and in their clothes. There is the mayor in his offical garb, and the fisherwoman with her basket full of catches from the sea. Roma (gypsies) appear in their colorful clothes and jewelry. A shepherd carries a lamb in his arms. The shepherdess stands beside him, perhaps chatting with the village gossip.

Many of the santons are arranged as though they are on their way to see Little Jesus in the manger. A drummer boy leads them, and a boy with a fife. Each santon carries a gift to offer the Christ Child: a chicken, a basket of fruit, some flowers. The gifts may not be as valuable as those of the Three Kings, also represented at the crèche. But the presents of the folk are far more touching. No one is excluded: the baker, the pastry maker, and the hunter, who turns aside his gun. Even thieves, and pickpockets may take their place in the crèche, making it a true representation of society.

The traditional Nativity animals—the ox, the lamb, the donkey—are joined by sheepdogs, rabbits, chickens, and other farmyard creatures. Sometimes, the santon makers create exotic animals. Camels, elephants, or a leopard or two may be seen among the other figures.

The history of the santons goes back to at least the 1600's. However, santon fairs, in which craftsmen sold santons they had made, began in the early 1800's, when a group of Italian peddlers came to Marseille. The peddlers brought with them the small, brightly painted figures made of clay, which they sold in the city's streets and markets.

Local artisans were so delighted with the figures that they began to make santons, too, in French dress of the period. Artisans have been doing so ever since, and their work is considered some of the finest in the world.

The exquisite details of painted santons reflect life in the French countryside in the 1800's. Of the two types of clay santons, the painted ones are the most beloved.

Making santons is a family occupation in Provence. Many santon makers are the product of several generations of artisans, from great-grandfather on down. Creating the figures is a painstaking art, taught by fathers and mothers to the youngsters, who assist after school and during vacations. First-generation santon makers are rare and have usually married into families of santon artisans.

The clay figures are molded in two halves; when they are pressed together, the clay fuses into a whole. Then the artist creates the appearance or expression desired. Such accessories as hats, baskets, and the tools of many trades are attached to the body with a special adhesive.

As the figure dries and hardens, it gradually changes color. When completely dry, it is given a bath in a solution of gelatin to harden it further and to give it a special gloss. This covering provides a good surface for the application of paint pigments. Without it, the colors would run.

Then the santons are lined up in rows, one type of character per row. All the millers will be together, for instance, or all the winemakers. Their faces are painted first, then the hair, the clothing, and any accessories.

Until the end of the 1800's, clay santons were not fired in kilns but merely dried in the sun. Even as late as 1945, many santon makers clung to the old open-air tradition. A few still do today. But the classic, old-style santons are so fragile that they tend to break, so most santon makers now fire them for longer life and durability.

Each year in Marseille, a special santon fair is held. There are not many santon makers, and only a few dozen come to set up their displays in Allées de Meilhan, the market spot where the fair takes place. Over 100 different types of painted and clothed santons may be exhibited at one stall—a full year's work. Each santon maker has a separate stand, with the family on hand to help with the sales.

Santons clothed in miniature versions of period dress move toward the manger, carrying their gifts for the Infant Jesus.

Many magnificent antique crèches with their lovely santons can be seen today in churches and in homes. Museums particularly treasure them and carefully preserve the crèches, bringing them out each year for all to admire.

The church at Le Beausset in Provence has a crèche more than 100 years old. Its santons are reunited only at Christmastime. The rest of the year, the treasured figures are scattered among the different families of the village, who care for them with great affection.

Another marvelous manger scene is at the church of Saint-Antoine de Ginestière, in Nice. The background is a miniature medieval castle, set on a mountaintop.

To be sure, there are crèches in France that differ from the traditional Provençal type. They are made of wood, paper, and porcelain. But, innovation aside, the French always go back to their favorite when thinking of the crèche as it should be: a place of simplicity, where everyone belongs. They think of the crèche of Provence. There, all the humble santons stand near the Christ Child, Who welcomes them all.

Thirteen Desserts and More

Réveillon, in many households, may end with a magnificent bûche de Noël. However, some families, particularly those in Provence, may offer their guests 13 desserts. For good luck in the coming year, one is supposed to sample some of each of the 13.

According to one tradition, the 13 desserts symbolize Christ and his 12 apostles at the Last Supper. Some of the desserts also have meanings of their own. The 13 desserts may include:

- black nougat (hard candy made with caramelized honey and roasted almonds), symbolizing evil;
- white nougat (soft candy made with honey and eggwhites), symbolizing good;
- dried fruits and nuts symbolizing the four religious orders of "holy beggars," that is, monks and nuns who renounced wealth to live and work among the poor:
  - dried figs, representing the Franciscans;
  - almonds, representing the Carmelites;
  - hazelnuts, representing the Augustinians;
  - raisins, representing the Dominicans;
- dates, symbolizing the safe journey of Mary and Joseph from the East;
- fresh fruit—including oranges, clementines, apples, pears, grapes, or apricots—depending on the region;
- candied chestnuts;
- winter melon candied in syrup;
- a flat pastry called "fougasse" in some provinces and "pompe à l'huile" in others.

A family may choose to have the bûche de Noël or the 13 desserts after the group has returned from midnight Mass. The 13 desserts are often left out for the next three days, until December 27, for all to enjoy. Then, everyone has a few days to relax and prepare for the next holiday, New Year's Eve.

The table has been carefully laid, and the 13 desserts await guests.

New Year's celebrations

The French consider Noël to be primarily a time for children, a time to be spent with family. But New Year's Eve and New Year's Day bring opportunities for adults to exchange gifts and to spend time with friends. Many families send New Year's cards—wishing friends health, prosperity, and joy in the coming year—rather than Christmas cards. New Year's Eve may find them at another elaborate réveillon. Often the New Year's Eve réveillon is timed to end just before midnight. Then, champagne flows and fireworks explode as everyone celebrates the beginning of the new year.

New Year's Day is often called Jour des Etrennes, Day of New Year's Presents. Adults exchange small gifts, such as chocolates, flowers, preserved fruits, and candied chestnuts. They may also tip those who perform services for the household during the year, such as mail carriers or shop keepers.

Families gather on New Year's Day for reunion dinners. These are often held at the home of the oldest family member.

Epiphany

The Christmas season ends, for most of the people of France, with the Epiphany, or the feast of Three Kings, on January 6. Epiphany commemorates the visit of the Three Wise Men, who came to Bethlehem bearing gifts for the newborn Jesus.

In Provence on Twelfth Night, the evening before Epiphany, children wait outside to watch for the Magi. If they see them passing, the children offer food to help the visitors on their way. In return, the Three Kings may present the children with small gifts.

On Three Kings day, families may enjoy a special pastry called the galette des Rois, or kings' cake. The galette is a round, flat pastry baked with a tiny porcelain trinket, an almond, or, most often, a dried bean called a *fève* inside. The cake is presented topped with a card-

Truffle growers hold a traditional auction of the culinary treats during the feast of Epiphany in Provence.

board crown. Whoever is served the piece containing the bean becomes king—or queen—for the day and wears the crown.

With the celebration of Epiphany, the season of Noël comes to an end. The decorations are taken down and carefully wrapped to be stored for another year. The tree is removed, and the people of France settle in for the remaining months of winter. But the joy of the season lingers, preserved in memories that can be brought to life in an instant with a single word, Noël.

Treats of Noël
Pompe à l'huile/Fougasse

3 ¾ cups all-purpose flour, sifted
⅓ cup plus 1 tbsp. sugar
1 7-gram package active dry yeast
¾ cup extra-virgin olive oil
2 tsp. salt
grated zest of 1 orange
1 tbsp. olive oil
powdered sugar (optional)

1. In a large bowl, combine 1 ½ cups of the flour with the sugar, yeast, and 1 cup of lukewarm water. Stir well with a wooden spoon. Let the mixture sit in a warm spot until bubbly, about 30 minutes.

2. Add remaining 2 ¼ cups flour, ¾ cup of the oil, salt, and orange zest to the large bowl. Stir until a dough forms. Turn the dough out onto a lightly floured surface and knead until smooth and elastic (5 to 7 minutes). Grease a large clean bowl with the 1 tbsp. olive oil, place dough in the bowl, and cover with a clean linen towel. Set the dough aside in a warm, draft-free spot to rise until doubled in bulk (3 to 4 hours).

3. Preheat oven to 400 °F. Carefully turn dough out onto a large sheet of parchment paper and gently stretch it with your fingers to form a 12" circle. Using a small, sharp knife, cut out five 2"-long slits, each about 1" wide, starting from the center of the bread and cutting toward the edge, so that the dough will resemble a sand dollar (discard dough scraps). Using your fingers, gently stretch the holes open a little wider. Carefully transfer the dough (still on the parchment paper) to a large baking sheet. Bake until golden brown and puffed (about 15 minutes). Remove the bread from the oven and immediately brush the top and sides with 2 tbsp. hot water to soften the crust. Transfer the bread to a rack to cool. If desired, sprinkle with powdered sugar before serving.

Yield: one loaf.

Black Nougat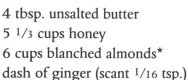

4 tbsp. unsalted butter
5 1/3 cups honey
6 cups blanched almonds*
dash of ginger (scant 1/16 tsp.)

1. Rub the butter on a marble pastry board. Set aside in a cool place, with newspapers under board to protect your work surface. Prepare a large glass of ice-cold water; set aside near stove.

2. Pour honey into a medium saucepan. Bring to a simmer, stirring constantly. Reduce heat to low and cook 10 minutes. Add almonds and ginger, and cook 15 to 30 minutes more, stirring constantly. Honey will begin to thicken and darken; nuts will darken. To test for doneness, drop a teaspoonful of honey into the prepared glass of ice-cold water; if ready, honey will form brittle threads immediately. (If using candy thermometer, mixture must reach 300 °F, or hard-crack stage.) Remove pan from heat.

3. Immediately, carefully pour honey/nut mixture onto prepared pastry board. Working quickly, smooth mixture with well-greased backs of 2 metal spoons or a well-greased rolling pin to spread evenly. (Be careful; mixture is very hot.) When nougat is completely cool, break it into 2" pieces. Store in a cool, dry place.

* To blanch almonds: Place raw, shelled almonds in bowl. (About 2 lbs. of shelled almonds will yield 6 cups of blanched almonds.) Cover just barely with boiling water; let stand about 2 minutes. Drain, then rinse under cold water until almonds are cool enough to handle. Pat dry and rub between fingers to remove skins.

Yield: about 5 lbs.

Galette des Rois

(King's Cake)

1 package (16 oz.) frozen puff pastry, thawed
1 egg
7 oz. pure almond paste, softened
(place in tall glass of warm water
for 5 minutes)

1 dried bean (kidney or great northern)
or 1 blanched almond
egg wash
(1 egg yolk mixed with 1 tbsp. milk)
1 cardboard or lightweight plastic crown

1. Preheat oven to 425 °F. Line a baking sheet with parchment paper; set aside.

2. In medium bowl, use electric mixer on low speed to mix 1 egg with the almond paste. Set aside.

3. Separate puff pastry sheets into two equal stacks. Set one aside.

4. Working in a cool place if possible, place the other stack on a sheet of waxed paper. Roll into an 11" square. Using a pie plate as a guide, trace an 11" circle in the pastry. Cut it out with tip of a sharp knife. Lay circle on parchment paper.

5. Repeat step 4 with the remaining puff pastry. With knife, trim second circle slightly smaller (about 10" in diameter).

6. Mound the almond paste mixture in the middle of the puff pastry on the parchment paper. Add the dried bean or almond. Use spatula to spread mixture toward edges of pastry, stopping ½" from edges.

7. With water, moisten exposed edges of pastry. Lay smaller stack of puff pastry over bottom stack. Fold up bottom pastry stack and crimp to seal. Brush top crust with egg wash. With sharp knife, draw criss-cross pattern across top. Prick top with fork in about 8 places so steam can escape during cooking. Bake 20 minutes, then lower heat to 400 °F and bake 15 minutes more or until golden brown. Serve warm. Place crown atop cake before serving.

Serves 8.

Homespun Treasures

Tricolored star

Materials

- pencil, tracing paper
- scissors, cardboard, hole punch
- 2 sheets each of red, green, white construction paper
- 4 inches x 4 inches piece clear vinyl or acetate (mylar)
- stapler
- 9 inches fine metallic cord
- 2 metal rings, 1/2-inch diameter
- pliers

pattern 1

1. Trace each of the three patterns on pages 72 and 73 onto tracing paper. Cut out patterns. Place patterns on cardboard. Outline and cut out. Use the largest cardboard pattern to outline and cut 8 pieces of each color of construction paper (8 red, 8 green, 8 white). Punch holes where indicated on pattern. Outline the two small pattern pieces onto vinyl and cut them out. Punch holes where indicated and put aside.

2. Place two large white pattern pieces aside. Divide other large pattern pieces in pairs of same color (4 red pairs, 4 green pairs, 3 white pairs). About 1/3 of the way up from the bottom of each pair, staple center together. Staple each pair together in identical spot.

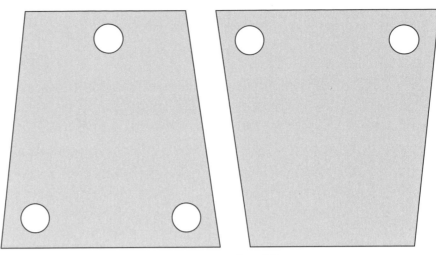

patterns 2 and 3

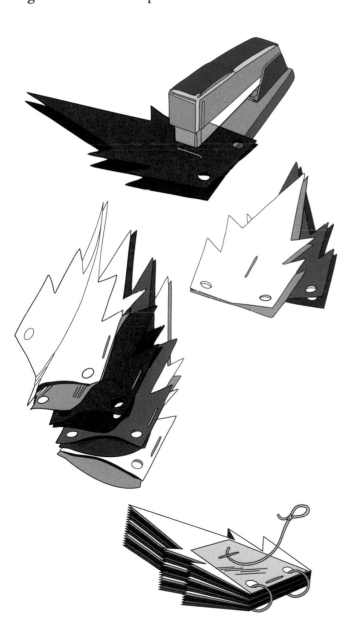

3. In color sequence, staple sides of individual pattern pieces together, stapling the bottom piece of one color pair to the top piece of the next color pair. Color sequence is red/green/white/red. Repeat, making sure corner holes line up evenly.

4. Assemble two extra white pattern pieces, two pieces of vinyl, and cord. Punch a hole near the top center of one piece of vinyl. Staple piece to one extra white pattern piece near top and bottom, making sure bottom holes line up. Repeat with other extra white pattern piece and vinyl, omitting hole punch step. Instead, with vinyl facing out, staple middle of cord to pieces. Tie loose end of cord into a knot. Vinyl facing out, staple two white pieces to other pieces at side, one at each end. Open metal rings with pliers. Put through all holes in pattern pieces, one ring each side. Close rings tightly with pliers.

5. Pull knotted end of cord through hole in vinyl at opposite end. Ornament will unfold into a decorative star.

Père Noël ornament/pin

Materials
- pencil, tracing paper
- scissors
- 5" x 8" colored felt rectangles, red and skin-colored (one each)
- straight pins
- needle
- thread, red, skin-colored
- 3 yards white rug or craft yarn
- scraps of black felt
- white glue
- cotton balls
- large safety pins

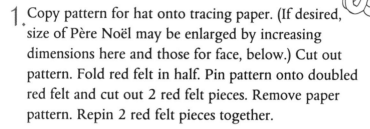

1. Copy pattern for hat onto tracing paper. (If desired, size of Père Noël may be enlarged by increasing dimensions here and those for face, below.) Cut out pattern. Fold red felt in half. Pin pattern onto doubled red felt and cut out 2 red felt pieces. Remove paper pattern. Repin 2 red felt pieces together.

2. Using red thread, sew red pieces together with a running stitch about ¼ inch from edge, leaving bottom open. For face pieces, repeat step 1 with skin-colored felt, sewing sides together and leaving top open. Sew bottom of hat to top of face in front only.

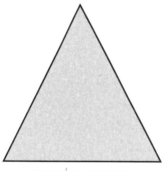

trace these patterns

3. For beard, take white rug yarn and make loops about 1 inch long. Stitch with white thread along edge of face. For features, cut out black felt eyes and red felt mouth. Use yarn for eyebrows. Attach features with white glue. For moustache, make a small bow of white yarn and sew on center of face.

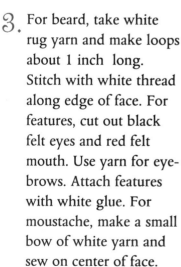

4. At open back, stuff hat and face loosely with cotton balls. Sew up back.

5. Glue cotton balls along front seam where hat joins face. Glue one cotton ball at top of hat for pompon. Sew base of large safety pin to back of hat. Nestle Père Noël in tree as ornament to be given to children as lapel decoration.

Kitchen clay fruit ornaments

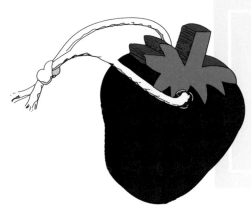

Materials:

- pencil
- tracing paper
- scissors
- mixing bowl
- mixing spoon
- 1 cup salt
- 2 cups flour
- ½ tsp. baking powder
- 1 cup water
- flour
- small knife
- toothpick
- tempera paints
- paintbrush
- clear nail polish
- decorative cord

1. Copy fruit patterns onto tracing paper. Cut out patterns.

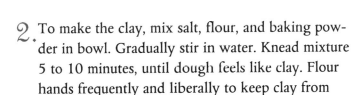

trace these patterns

2. To make the clay, mix salt, flour, and baking powder in bowl. Gradually stir in water. Knead mixture 5 to 10 minutes, until dough feels like clay. Flour hands frequently and liberally to keep clay from sticking. Yields 3 cups.

3. Sprinkle flour liberally on work surface and hands. Take a small lump of clay and roll it into a ball between your hands. Flatten clay ball evenly with palm to ⅜-inch thickness.

4. Place fruit pattern on flattened clay. Using knife, cut around edge. Remove pattern. With toothpick, draw interior details on fruit and make a hole near the top of fruit. Hole must be large enough to avoid closing up during drying. Repeat for other fruit patterns. If desired, create some original fruit or other ornament patterns for use with remaining clay.

5. Allow ornaments to air-dry for at least 48 hours. Paint ornaments. Allow ornaments to dry thoroughly again. Seal with coat of clear nail polish. Cut one 8-inch piece of cord for each ornament. Thread cord through hole. Knot ends together. Use cord to hang ornaments on tree.

Sing Noël

Sleep, Little Jesus

Entre le boeuf et l'âne gris

Andante
13th Century

En-tre le boeuf et l'â-ne gris, dors, dors, dors le pe-tit fils -

mille an -ges di – vins, mil-le sé -ra — phins, vo-lent à l'en — tour de ce grand Dieu-

—— d'a — mour ————

Ox and gray donkey bring Thee laud,
Sleep, sleep, little Lamb of God.
Angels all in rhyme, thousands at a time,
Sing to Thee, oh God of Love,
Emmanuel divine.

Near rose and lily white as pearl,
Sleep, sleep, Savior of our world.
Angels in the sky, sing Thy lullaby,
Slumber in Thy manger,
Son of God on high.

Shepherds have come the Babe to find,
Sleep, sleep, hope of humankind.
Angels sing on high, shepherds pray nearby.
All is safe, so little Jesus
Close Thy eyes.

Christ Is Born, Play the Music, Sing!

Il est né, le divin Enfant

Allegretto
Traditional

Refrain:
Christ is born, play the music, sing!
Bring out the pipes, beat the drum, together.
Christ is born, play the music, sing!
Raise your voices to praise our King.

Long ago in the Promised Land,
Prophets told of a Savior reigning.
Long ago in the Promised Land,
Christ the Lord came from heaven's hand.
(Refrain)

Humbly placed on a bed of straw,
Christ was born in a lonely stable.
Humbly placed on a bed of straw,
Christ the King came to save us all.
(Refrain)

Shout His glory and raise His song,
Pauper and prince hail the Son, your Savior.
Shout His glory and raise His song.
Join the praise of the mighty throng.
(Refrain)

Oh, Holy Night

Minuit, Chrétiens

Adolphe Adam

Largetto

Mi-nuit, chré-tiens, c'est l'heure so-len-nel-le où l'homme Dieu descen-dit jusqu'à nous pour ef-fa

-cer — la tache o - ri - gi — nel — le et de son Père ar-rê — ter le cour — roux ———— le

monde en-tier tres — sail-le d'es-pé - ran - ce en cette nuit qui lui don - ne un sau—veur-

REFRAIN

Peuple   à ge - noux ———— at-tends ———— ta dé - li —vran - ce No — ël ———— No -

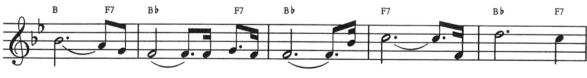

-ël ———— Voi - ci ———— le rédemp - teur ———— No — ël ———— No — ël ———— Voi -

-ci ——— le rédemp ——— teur.

Oh, holy night, the stars are brightly shining,
It is the night of the dear Savior's birth.
Long lay the world in sin and error pining,
Till He appeared and the soul felt its worth.
A thrill of hope, the weary world rejoices,
For yonder breaks a new and glorious morn.
   Fall on your knees!
   Oh, hear the angel voices!
   Oh, night divine;
   Oh, night when Christ was born.
   Oh, night divine!
   Oh, night, Oh, night divine!

Led by the light of faith serenely beaming,
With glowing hearts by His cradle we stand;
So led by light of a star sweetly gleaming,
Here came the Wise Men from Orient land.
The King of Kings lay thus in lowly manger,
In all our trials born to be our friend.
   He knows our need,
   To our weakness is no stranger.
   Behold your King!
   Before Him lowly bend!
   Behold your King!
   Before Him lowly bend!

Truly He taught us to love one another;
His law is love, and His gospel is peace.
Chains shall He break, for the slave is our brother,
And in His name all oppressions shall cease.
Sweet hymns of joy in grateful chorus raise we,
Let all within us praise His holy name.
   Christ is the Lord,
   Oh, praise His name forever!
   His power and glory
   Evermore proclaim!
   His power and glory
   Evermore proclaim!

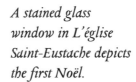

A stained glass window in L'église Saint-Eustache depicts the first Noël.

Acknowledgments

Cover: © Ingram Publishing/SuperStock
2: © Marc Bertrand
6: © Cephas Picture Library/Alamy Images
8: Dennis Mansell
10: © Arco Images GmbH/Alamy Images
11: © Marc Bertrand;
© Stockfolio/Alamy Images
12: © Robert Fried
13: WORLD BOOK photo by Joe Viesti;
© Gaston Malherbe/Louis Mercier
14: © Danita Delimont, Alamy Images
15: © MAXPPP/Landov
16: © J. J. Damiani
17: © Directphoto/Alamy Images
18: © Stefan Ataman, Shutterstock;
© Amelie Dupont
19: © Tim Graham, Alamy Images
20: © Herve Donnezan, Photo
Researchers
21: © Gaston Malherbe/Louis Mercier
22: © Masterfile
24: © Gaston Malherbe/Louis Mercier
25: © Bajande, Photo Researchers
26: © Danita Delimont, Alamy Images
27: © Robert Fried
28: © Danita Delimont, Alamy Images
30: © Stuart Crump, Alamy Images
31: © Reunion de Musees Nationaux
(Art Resource)
32: Art Resource
33-34: Historical Pictures Service, Inc.
35: Rigal/Editions Arthaud, Paris
36: © Amelie Dupont
38: © B. C. Press/Photo Researchers
39: Granger Collection
41: © Owen Franken
42: © J. J. Damiani
43: © J. J. Damiani, Photo Researchers

44-45: © Bertrand Rieger, Hemis
46: © SnowyWelsh/Alamy Images
48-49: WORLD BOOK photo by Joe Viesti
50: © Rapho, Photo Researchers
51: © Rapho, Photo Researchers;
© Serrailler, Photo Researchers
52-53: © Bertrand Rieger, Hemis
54: © Andia/Digital Railroad
55: © Bertrand Rieger, Hemis
56: © Gaston Malherbe/Louis Mercier
57: WORLD BOOK photo by
Joe Viesti; © J. J. Damiani
58: WORLD BOOK photo by Joe Viesti
59: © Andia/Digital Railroad
61: © Owen Franken
62: © Stockfolio/Alamy Images
63: © Jaubert Bernard, Alamy Images
64: WORLD BOOK photo by Free Chin
65: © Halin, Photo Researchers
67: © Photononstop/Alamy Images
68: © Patrick Frilet, Hemis
69-71: WORLD BOOK photos by
Karen Ingebretsen
79: © Patrick Ward, Alamy Images

Craft Illustrations: James M. Curran

Advent Calendar:
© Remy de la Mauviniere, AP Wide World

Advent Calendar Illustrations and
Recipe Cards: Eileen Mueller Neill

All maps and illustrations are exclusive
property of World Book, Inc.

The story "The Christmas Rose" (pages 10-11)
is adapted from Maguelonne Toussaint-Samat,
Légendes et récits du temps de Noël (Paris: Fernand
Nathan, Editeur 1977).